Poems Fr
Imagination...

Judith Blatherwick

ISBN: 1537698095
ISBN-13: 978-1537698090

DEDICATION

For all of my family and friends.

CONTENTS

ACKNOWLEDGMENTS

With thanks to Gary, Tom, Wes, Kelly, Annette, Donna and all of my PH friends for their encouragement and support.

Special thanks to Woodland Trust Scotland for allowing me to use Pressmennan Fairies. Pressmennan Wood, East Lothian is truly a magical place.

Fairytale

I want a world of fairies,
Of great alchemy and spells.
I want a world where heroes
Always vanquish ne'er-do-wells.

I want a world where maidens,
With their locks, so long and fair,
Stare out from lofty towers
Hoping that their knights are there.

I want to see a unicorn
Step shyly from the trees,
And as it sees me watching
Turn to gold dust on the breeze.

I'd like to have three wishes
Gifted to me by a witch.
I'd like to weave a new world
Made from magic, stitch by stitch.

I'd love to see a griffin
Flying way up in the sky.
Or spot a distant dragon
And hide as it passes by.

I want to plant a plum tree
And grow silver and gold fruits,
Then look down and see tree nymphs
Hiding in between the roots.

How nice to see a mermaid
Swim with grace out in a lake,
Then turn to see a princess
Just being kissed to make her wake.

I know the world I wish for
May make me seem slightly fey,

So I'll leave it in my dream world
And live in this one by day.

Moonbeam

I swear tonight it touched me.
In the wonder of the night,
As the stars stood by to witness
I felt bathed in silver light.

In the stillness and the silence
I closed my eyes to wait.
Its coolness washed across me.
When I looked it was too late.

But I knew at once, it touched me.
It sent down one tender beam.
It touched, then left me breathless.
Or perhaps it was a dream.

Magic By Nature

You can almost hear the bluebells ring.
Those little drops of sky.
They sway with grace and beauty
As the gentle breeze goes by.

Look at the laburnum,
Pendants of the finest gold.
Nature's chest of riches
For the whole world to behold.

Bridesmaid's gowns of lilac
And a cherry blossom bride.
Church candles on the chestnut trees,
Below, shy violets hide.

Military tulips stand
In tunics of bright red.
Below them pansies nodding,
Each one with a smiling head.

Tell me there's no magic
In the world in which we live.
And then explain the beauty
Of what nature has to give.

For magic, at its finest,
Works enchantments and casts spells.
So tell me, without magic
How can we explain bluebells.

Circus Of Lost Souls

You're welcome, Gents and Ladies,
To the first of my new shows.
What will happen in them?
Well, I have to say, who knows?

Amongst the great attractions
We have people with great gifts.
You'll see tremendous feats of
Balance, courage, mighty lifts.

This is a magic circus.
Are the artists from this world?
We know we'll see you gasping
As our talents are unfurled.

So roll up, roll up people.
Buy your ticket at the door.
It's time our great performers
Bring their talents to the fore.

First on, our ballerina,
Who performs with fairy grace.

She dances on a tightrope
Made from silken spider's lace.

Next out, our clown, so cheerful
With a false grin and red nose.
Behind his cheeky makeup
Is he evil? No-one knows.

Up on the high trapeze
Performers watch you from above.
For them to swing so freely
Are there talons 'neath each glove?

And to our haunting music,
Wafting gently through the air.
Can you all see the musicians?
No? Perhaps they are not there.

So roll up, roll up, one and all.
The circus has arrived.
You may have heard about us
From the people who've survived.

For we are all unhindered
By convention and by rules.
You want to join this circus?
We will always accept fools.

For we are soul collectors,
We are spirits in your midst.
And if you choose to join us,
You'll remain here. We insist.

So all of you are welcome!
Get your ticket at the door.
The only cost is your soul.
You won't need it any more.

A Child And Her Moth

She was pretty as a picture,
Sugar sweet. And terrified.
She gazed up at the nightlight
Where no evil things could hide.

She was quite brave in day time,
But night terrors ran so deep.
Without her trusty nightlight
She would never get to sleep.

She glanced around her bedroom.
Feeling sleepy, she lay down.
But as she heard a tapping
Her small face turned to a frown.

She opened her eyes quickly.
Need to look, don't want to see.
She couldn't sleep till she knew
What the tapping sound could be.

Around her dim light fluttered
A small creature of the night.
A pale and ghostly spectre,
Wings of dust and glowing white.

She gasped and snapped her eyes shut,
Pulled the quilt above her head.
Then a voice of sunshine
Sounded right next to her bed.

'Don't be afraid my sweetheart,
I'm not here to do you harm.
I guard you as you're sleeping.
There's no need for your alarm.

I search the room for monsters,
Keep the scarey things away.
Protecting you from shadows

Till I'm born again next day.'

'But what are you? ' she whispered,
'I'm a butterfly, my dear.
If you saw me in daylight
I know you would have no fear'.

'But butterflies are rainbows.
They are cheerful, they are bright.
You are dull and faded.
You are darkness. They are light'.

The butterfly laughed softly.
'I know that is how it seems.
At night I give my colour
To bring beauty to your dreams.

Come morning I start changing.
I'm reborn and I'm made new.
I earn my right to colour
As I watch and protect you.

So sleep now. I am watching.
Nothing bad is hiding here.
Sweet dreams my little lady.
You are safe. I will be near'.

Royal Houses Of Light And Dark

In a misty state of nothing,
With no form yet to the skies,
Two ancient royal houses
Bellowed out their battle cries.

This mighty clash of armies
Fought beneath an ancient curse.
The war had raged for eons.
The prize, the universe.

With a blazing golden banner
Fought the Royal House of Light.
Their King rode out before them,
Golden armour burning bright

The Royal House of Darkness
By their mighty King was led.
In burnished silver armour,
Riding fiercely at their head.

Time and space suspended
As the bloody war tides turned.
At times the dark was victor.
And at others bright light burned.

In one small space of nothing
The Light and Dark Kings met.
Both drew their swords of power,
And the battle lines were set.

'For Light! ' the gold King shouted
As his sword flashed through the mist.
The jewel encrusted hilt clenched firmly
In his bloodied fist.

'For Dark! ' A sword of silver
Slashed to meet the sword of Light.
The gemstone handle shuddered
As it met its foe with might.

In combat that was brutal
These two mighty kings engaged.
Around them, in the nowhere,
Many bitter battles raged.

But with both great kings equal,
Neither could the other beat.
And neither would give way
And call their army to retreat.

As their swords crashed fiercely
The empty sky was filled
With jewels and precious gemstones
Which from damaged hilts were spilled.

The battle ground moved onwards
Through the never ending space.
The jewel and gemstone wreckage
Settled gently into place.

The sapphires sparkled brightly.
Stars of bright blue in the night
A pearl of purest beauty
With a gentle cooling light.

A citrine of bright yellow
Blazed with power from the war.
Imbibed with fervent passion
It shone brightly from its core.

And spinning in this somewhere
Was a gemstone of great worth.
A perfect blue green opal.
And this stone became the Earth.

Whizzy Izzy

A magical fairy who so loved to fly
Would flutter around through the flowers.
She never got tired and others asked why
She was able to waste all those hours.

The others had jobs they must do every day;
So why should she be the exception?
Their jealousy meant, when she passed by their way
They gave her a chilly reception.

The Union of Fairies (which she was not in)
Approached the Chief Fairy complaining.

But before their moaning could even begin
He launched into some lengthy explaining.

"This fairy, I know, seems exempt from the rules,
Just fluttering round without working.
And you're sure that you are being taken for fools,
While I tolerate her and her shirking.

But surely you've seen as she's flying around
That she stops at each flower and mutters.
If you've taken note I am sure that you've found
All the blooms listen to what she utters.

For though you may think that her life is a breeze
Her work is in fact very vital.
The fact that she loves it and does it with ease
Means she doesn't want any posh title.

She whispers to flowers and asks them to grow,
So we can enjoy their great beauty.
What does she whisper? I really don't know,
But she does it for love and not duty.

So when you admire a Stock or a Rose,
Or a Bluebell or bright Busy Lizzie,
Don't glare at or bully or turn up your nose
At the fairy who's called Whizzy Izzy."

Demon Hunting

You can't see me, but you feel me.
Icy fingers down your spine.
I know you know I'm watching.
Those soft whispers? They are mine.

My coldness passes through you.
I can touch your very soul.
Your life force keeps me nourished,
Though on you this takes its toll.

Your energy sustains me,
I feed deeply on your fear.
I thirst for those brief moments
When you feel me standing near.

For the moment you're protected,
But I'm waiting for a sign.
For I'm a demon hunting,
And on Hallowe'en you're mine.

Candle Magic

A bouquet of candles
Lies here where I sit.
A rainbow of magic
Is soon to be lit.

I cast with intentions
Of causing no harm
I cast with the colours
Of love, peace and calm.

I light green
For abundance, good luck and success.
For you, my good friend
I would wish nothing less.

I light yellow
For wisdom, endurance and trust.
If you're to be happy,
These three are a must.

I light red
For your courage, great passion and fire.
May these bring a life
Which is rich with desire.

I light pink

For devotion and friendship, romance.
When you find all of these
Do not fear. Take the chance.

I light gold
For protection, for safety and care.
Should you ever need me,
Just look. I'll be there..

I light orange
To bring to you only good things.
To soften the pain
When you suffer life's stings.

I light blue
To bring harmony and give you peace.
For loyalty and wisdom.
For anguish to cease.

I light white
For enlightenment, cleansing and hope,
To strengthen your spirit
So you always cope.

So now they are lit,
And the spell cast by me.
May your life be a wonder
My friend. Blessed Be.

A Rainbow Candle For Gary

Just one candle remains,
And its flame I will light
May the magic cross miles
To make your future bright.

This candle is special.
A colourful blend,
To bring luck and good fortune

To one special friend.

Now the candle is lit,
The enchantment complete.
May the magic it brings you
Make your lifetime sweet.

Fairies In My Garden

I've fairies in my garden.
I saw them in the moonlight.
Their wings sparkled with magic
Where silver beams shone most bright.

A mother fairy rode through
The borders on a spider.
Her baby in a leaf-crib
Rode on a bug beside her.

Two reckless youths were fencing
With blades of grass for swords.
A young girl on a fern harp
Sang along to haunting chords.

Two gentlemen of some age
Smoked pipes of acorn shells,
While their good ladies sipped tea
Out of upturned bright bluebells.

Two beauties giggled softly
As they hid behind a rose.
Their laughter was a tinkling
As they talked about their beaus.

I know that they can't see me
So I take the chance to stare.
For if I look away, when
I look back they wont be there.

I've fairies in my garden.
I tell you it is true!
And if you're a believer
They may appear for you.

Now you might think I'm crazy,
But I'll tell you how I know.
I asked the gnomes who live there
And they told me it was so.

Grandad's Moustache

My Grandad was a great man;
Very kind but still quite stern.
He didn't give us handouts.
All we got we had to earn.

The war had shaped his facade.
He had been a flying ace.
He stood up tall and dashing
A bushy moustache graced his face.

He twirled it when deep thinking.
He twirled through war and truce.
And I am quite convinced that
With this twirling it came loose.

For once I spent an evening
Watching Grandad take a nap.
He twirled his 'tash while sleeping
And it dropped onto his lap!

It twitched there upon landing
Then it dropped onto the floor.
It ran across the carpet.
I could see the 'tash no more.

I heard it in the shadows
As it skittered in the dark.

I tried to wake my Grandad,
But he'd gone out like a spark.

I stared at Grandad sleeping
While his moustache took a trip.
His hand reached up and Grandad
Scratched his unmoustached top lip.

Then suddenly his moustache,
Having had its exercise,
Ran from beneath the sideboard
Right beneath my very eyes.

It climbed up onto Grandad,
And it took its rightful place.
It wiggled and it parked up
On my Grandad's naked face.

Grandad woke up shortly,
And he saw me as I stared.
I must admit I looked shocked
As I felt a little scared.

I told him what had happened,
How his 'tash had run about.
His glare was quite unyielding.
I expected him to shout.

But Grandad barely whispered
As he told me I was wrong.
He'd never lost his moustache,
He had had it for so long.

But I was quite insistent;
Knew exactly what I'd seen.
I pointed to the sideboard
Under which the 'tash had been.

He looked into the mirror,
Stroked his 'tash and gave a frown.

Then turned to me, quite puzzled,
For his 'tash was upside down!

Gravity Of The Situation

"Can you please get back on your side"
Said the beach to the great sea.
"Your bed is huge already,
Do you have to push at me? "

"I know I test your patience"
Said the water to the sand.
"And I know I am a fidget
As I spread across your land.

But try to keep your temper.
I'll move back again quite soon.
If that is not sufficient
Send complaints up to the moon."

"Hey Moon! " the sand called loudly
"Is it really you to blame?
I can't see the connection,
But I'm fed up all the same! "

The moon, who had been listening
Called out, "Sand, for what it's worth,
The reason that this happens?
I'm attracted to the Earth!

As I travel round her
She is always moving too.
The gravity we both have means that
Sea, I pull on you.

If you wish to stop the movement

Then the Earth you must address.
But it would be much better
To accept the sea's caress."

The Earth then interrupted
"You are kidding! You must be!
The blame for all this movement
Lies with one greater than me.

Do you think that I keep spinning
For amusement? Just for fun?
If I gave up my dodging
We'd be sucked into the sun!

Do you know how hot the sun is?
Well, exactly, I've no clue.
But I know one thing for certain
It's no place for me or you!

My habits won't be changing,
So when all is said and done,
Express your great displeasure,
If you dare, straight to the sun."

The sun joined the debating
"I'm to blame, there is no doubt.
These issues would be sorted
If you chose to put me out.

But don't make hasty choices,
Which would only make things worse.
If I do not keep burning
Conditions will become adverse.

The first thing would be darkness.
You may say that's not so bad,

But eternity so gloomy?
That is sure to drive you mad.

Next thing would be the cooling.
I know that would not please you.
But if you put me out you'll freeze.
There's nothing I can do.

I guarantee the world will die.
You will all turn to ice.
Imagine how you'd all feel then.
It wouldn't be too nice."

The beach, the sea, the moon, the Earth
Fell silent at the news.
Given those two choices
Each one knew what they would choose.

"Step across my borders"
Said the beach to the great sea.
"Don't worry you're intruding.
There is room for you and me."

Stone Angel

The angel stands weeping,
Her head in her hands.
In perpetual mourning
Her vigil she stands.

Ever trapped in the moment,
She waits all alone.
A figure of heartbreak
Carved from time worn grey stone.

No-one left to remember.
All those memories lost.

But this weeping angel
Waits, whatever the cost.

The ivy grows thickly,
It inflicts wounds so deep.
But it isn't the pain
Which makes this angel weep.

Beneath where she's standing
A young woman lies.
It is for this poor girl
That the stone angel cries.

The writing, eroded,
Worn out and unclear,
Once told of the life
Of a loved one held dear.

Just 'Taken too young'
Are the words that remain.
While others surrendered
To wind and the rain.

Only one other word
Has passed Time's brutal test.
'Lucy' stands out
Clearer than all the rest.

Until that word fades
The stone angel will grieve.
When it's no longer there
She will quietly leave.

The angel of light
Will be freed from her task.
No longer needing
Her stone angel mask.

Judgement Day

"All silence in the courtroom"
Cried Court Officer Jackdaw.
"All stand" he ordered loudly
As Judge Eagle took the floor.

The Jackdaw bowed as Eagle
Took position on the bench.
A tweeting from the gallery
Saw Jackdaw's black beak clench.

"All sit" the Jackdaw ordered,
"And keep silent, show respect.
Swift justice for such twittering
Is what you can expect."

The Swift up in the gallery
Looked round, his guilt on show.
He'd tweeted when the others did,
But how did Jackdaw know?

Judge Eagle was resplendent in
His feathered gown of gold.
With sharp beak and his piercing eyes
His look was icy cold.

"Court Officer, the charges,
Read them clearly to the court."
"My Lord, here stands the Magpie
Who took things he hadn't bought."

The Judge stared at the Magpie, and
His face was stern and grim.
There was no doubt the Magpie knew
The charge applied to him.

"The charge you face is serious.
Now I will hear your plea.
Guilty or Not Guilty? Give your

Answer now to me."

The Magpie stared straight at him
And he had to swallow hard.
"My Lord, I am quite guiltless.
Please release me from this guard."

The Owl, for Prosecution, stood
And faced the Eagle Judge.
"Magpie must be punished, and
On this I will not budge."

He turned to face the Magpie and
Said "I have heard your plea.
I also saw you swallow.
That suggests a lie to me."

In the public gallery
A Swallow gave a hiss.
"The Magpie works alone" he said,
"Don't bring me into this."

The Crow, defending Magpie,
Stood and spoke (with a slight slur)
"M'lud, my client's innocent.
Please listen to him Sir."

"Robbin' is illegal. Magpie
Wouldn't get involved.
The evidence was planted,
This case hasn't yet been solved."

A Robin flapped and called out
"I am not against the law!
In fact I'm very much loved.
Don't say such things any more! "

"Cease the interruptions! " cried
Judge Eagle to the crowd.
He grabbed a passing Woodpecker

Who pecked the bench, quite loud.

"Do we have a witness who
Saw Magpie at this crime?
If so, then Owl produce him,
For we haven't got much time."

The Owl stood up, dejected,
No such witness did exist.
He thought the case was proven.
Jewels were found in Magpie's fist.

"No Sir we do not have one.
Magpie's much too smart for that.
Though when he was arrested
Stolen goods filled where he sat."

"Circumstantial evidence! "
The Crow cried "I insist
If there is not a witness
Then this case should be dismissed! "

The Judge thought Magpie guilty,
But was neutral all the same.
"Though Magpie had the jewellery
We don't know from where it came."

The jury (twelve good pigeons)
Listened to the evidence.
To come to a conclusion
They must use their common sense.

Meanwhile a ray of sunshine
Shone down on them from above.
A silver leg ring sparkled
On the leg of a white Dove.

The Magpie's dark eye twinkled
As he saw how bright it shone.
And with a rush of feathers

White Dove's silver ring was gone.

"Guilty! " cried the whole court
As the Magpie flew up high.
This time he had escaped them,
But his judgement day was nigh.

Moon Mystery

The Guardians of Nighttime
Settled high up in the trees.
Their feathers ruffled lightly
In the gentle summer breeze.

The Parliament had gathered,
Several owls, all of them wise.
They gazed up to the heavens
With their bright and knowing eyes.

"My friends, we don't meet lightly,
Our situation' s dire.
And only we can solve it,
As at night we don't retire."

The owl turned his eyes skywards,
Others following his gaze.
The moon above looked smaller
Than it had on prior days.

"I need to hear suggestions.
How can we put this right?
The moonlight is important
To the creatures of the night.

"I've studied this quite closely,
And I don't want you to scoff.
But this is my conclusion;
Part of the moon fell off."

In shock the owls looked upwards,
And were stunned by what they found.
It seemed a piece was missing.
It no longer looked as round.

"I know you are in shock now,
But I think that we should start.
Let's fly above the landscape.
We may find the missing part.

"We'll meet again tomorrow.
The moon may be good as new.
But if there's no improvement
We'll decide what we should do."

The owls took up the mission.
They took off and flew around.
They hoped they'd find the moonstone
Which had fallen to the ground.

They met again next evening,
Each of them was feeling low.
Once more the moon looked smaller
With a slightly dimmer glow.

"I've thought this through" said one owl,
"And I think the answer might
Be that a monstrous creature
Feeling hungry, took a bite"

They thought about this theory,
And the owls concluded soon
That if they didn't stop it
This beast might eat the whole moon.

All birdlife was enlisted
To search for it in daylight.
The Parliament was recalled
To discuss again that night.

"The search was quite extensive.
No moon-eating beast was found.
And as I'm sure you've noticed,
The moon is once again less round."

The owls all stared in silence.
They had no clue what they should do.
The moon above was shrinking.
What would happen? No-one knew.

Each night when they all gathered,
As they stared no-one dared blink.
They could find no solution,
Helplessly they watched it shrink.

Then one night just a fragment
Of the moon seemed to remain.
They pulled themselves together
And tried hard to think again.

An Eagle Owl stepped forward
And said "Nobody mock me.
I think I know the answer,
And it's simple as can be.

"The moon must get quite dirty,
I think that assumption's fair.
Perhaps we just can't see it,
Although it is still right there.

"It may be just that moondust
Has obscured it from our view,
And with a little cleaning
It may polish up like new.

"So this is my proposal.
To restore a bright moon lustre,
I'm going to fly up there and take
Some polish and a duster."

The owls met every twilight
And stared upwards all night through.
Eager to discover how
The eagle owl would do.

And slowly as the nights passed
The bright moon began to grow.
The eagle owl sprayed polish
As the rest watched from below.

Then one night as it darkened
They saw that the moon, restored,
Shone round and bright and silver,
And they cheered and laughed and roared.

The eagle owl returned home
And declared that the owls must
Fly to the moon once monthly
To remove the excess dust

Pyjama Tormentors

They have always seemed so harmless.
So friendly; not prone to attack.
Why then have my best pyjamas
Just lately begun to fight back?

For years I have managed to don them
One leg at a time with such ease.
But now both legs seem to evade me,
Leaving me puffed with a wheeze.

Each night I prepare for a battle,
Sure this time they won't pull a stunt.
Then just when I think I am winning
The trousers turn round back to front.

And meanwhile the jacket is laughing
As I feel defeated and grieve.
It knows if the trousers can't beat me
It has its own trick up its sleeve.

For one arm goes in with no bother,
I start to think that I may win,
But then, though I can see the other,
That sleeve will not let my arm in.

How have I offended my nightwear,
That they should torment me this way?
I dread every night as they taunt me.
So I've just one thing left to say.

'Pyjamas, you clearly don't like me.
And now my feelings are hurt.
So now I am going to reject you.
I'm buying a friendly night shirt.'

That Rat

A glimpse was all I saw at first.
A fleeting one at that.
It took a while to register
That I had seen a rat.

I peeped into the hole to see
If it was still about.
Imagine my surprise to find
That it was peeping out.

We sized up one another then,
The atmosphere intense.
We both squared up our shoulders.
Time for combat to commence.

Now to the local hardware store.
My weapons must be bought.
No room for sentiment in this.
Our battle must be fought.

Armed to the teeth I headed home.
That rat was going down.
But as I headed to my door
My smile changed to a frown.

The rat was sitting, bold as brass,
Beside the garden fence.
As I approached he didn't run.
He didn't even tense!

I dropped my bags and yelled at him
And gave my hands a clap.
"I'm ready now! You wont last long
'Cos I have bought a trap! "

Trap duly primed and loaded up
With rat attracting food,
I felt I had already won
And this improved my mood.

Next morning I rushed out to see
If my great plan had worked.
The food was gone, the trap was sprung.

The rat sat near. It smirked.

"Beginner's luck" I shouted out,
Convinced it couldn't last.
I threw a stone, but missed of course.
The rat was far too fast.

Each night I had another try,
It always was the same.
The rat, he wasn't giving in.
He seemed to love this game.

Battle fatigue was setting in.
I couldn't beat that rat.
He wasn't dead. In fact it seemed
That rat was getting fat.

I watched the rat. The rat watched me.
I tried to read his mind.
A strange thought formed inside my head
"He thinks I'm being kind."

Amazed was I when he reached out
And beckoned me outside.
This gesture, although very strange,
Could not have been denied.

So there we stood, me facing him.
His whiskers twitched. He spoke.
My jaw dropped and my eyes popped out,
Sure this was one big joke.

"I'd like to thank you for the food

You leave for me each night,
Although that dish is dangerous.
It gives me such a fright.

Can I do something nice for you,
To show you how I feel?
You're good to me and I'm nice back.
That is a friendly deal."

One thought popped straight into my mind.
No need to search for more.
"I'd take it as a friendly sign
If you could move next door."

The Battle

I couldn't get to sleep last night.
The world around felt sad.
The news I'd watched on TV
Showed no good, it just showed bad.

The wars and death and hate I'd seen
Festered in my mind.
The darkness overwhelmed me.
There seemed no light to find.

Was this the way it all would end?
Had mankind tolled the bell?
Instead of reaching Heaven
We have mimicked Satan's Hell.

And yet, across the world there are
So many more like me,

Who'd like to wash the grime away
And set the goodness free.

I drifted into fretful sleep,
An answer still not found.
But somewhere in my dream world I
Could hear a soothing sound.

The gentle beating of great wings
Preceded a great sight.
Seven mighty figures settled,
Bathed in golden light.

A fleeting fear engulfed me as
I wondered what were these.
A strong, yet soothing voice spoke out
"My child, please be at ease".

"We know that you are troubled, as
We know what all men think.
But we are here to tell you that
We'll pull Man from the brink.

"Archangels you may call us,
And although we may be few
We blaze a trail of glory
And our powers will save you".

Though fear had left me frozen
And my voice was low and weak,
I gazed upon the Seven and
I found that I could speak.

"Forgive me as I doubt you,
But I fail to understand,
How can you win this battle
With no weapons in your hand?

Although you are the greatest of
The great Angelic Host,
I fear that 'being good's'
The only weapon you can boast."

The first of the Archangels
Stepped forward from the rest.
"We're here to reassure you
That our weapons are the best.

I'm Archangel Michael,
And I bear a flaming sword.
I use it as a fighter,
Cutting paths through Satan's hoard."

The second one stepped forward
And he held my frightened gaze.
"Raphael I'm known as.
I can help in many ways.

I have the gift of healing
Of the spirit, body, mind.
When evil has been cast out
I will heal those left behind".

The third said "You may know me
For my name has been rejoiced.
I'm Archangel Gabriel.

Great messages I've voiced.

With great news I'm entrusted.
Divine messenger am I.
When victory is looming
I'll proclaim it from on high".

"Uriel is my name" the
Fourth Archangel cried.
"My gift is that of wisdom,
And I carry it with pride.

Pure evil can be clever,
But we'll win if we are wise.
I know what we are fighting.
I can see through its disguise."

Seraphiel walked forward
"Pure love is my special gift.
When evil rips hearts open
I am here to heal the rift.

I'll lift Man from his sorrows
And plant peace within your soul.
When you feel you're despairing
I will make your spirit whole"

Zophiel was the sixth one.
"I will help with a new start.
For my great gifts are beauty.
I am guardian of art.

So when the battle's over

And the darkness starts to clear
I'll be there to enlighten you
To all the beauty here".

The seventh, known as Raguel,
Said "I am both Just and Fair.
I battle for the underdogs.
When courage fails, I'm there.

So call me when you're needy,
And my justice will be true.
If you are not found wanting
I'll do battle to help you".

A final voice swept over
"In this battle that men face
I send my greatest angels
To protect the human race".

The light within my dream world
Faded to a dusky haze.
With seven great Archangels
We'll find peace in future days.

The Ballad Of Purdy And Alf

Purdy was a pampered cat;
She spent her days indoors.
She slept on soft upholstery
And walked on carpet floors.

Alfie was a hobo cat;
A proper bit of rough.

He strutted streets with attitude
His life was free but tough.

Purdy ate from china plates.
Her owner loved her so.
Alfie ate what he could get,
His expectations low.

But as the evening time drew on
And night time stole the sun
Both Alf and Princess Purdy stretched
And headed out for fun.

Purdy slunk through shadows,
Keeping low, eyes open wide.
Prepared, should there be danger,
To find somewhere safe to hide.

Alfie, such a street cat,
Didn't walk around in fear.
His growl proclaimed his presence
Should an enemy draw near.

Then one night in the shadows
Alfie spied some amber eyes.
They pulled back in the darkness.
Confrontation wasn't wise.

Purdy looked at Alfie,
And she felt a little fear.
She'd seen this wild cat often,
But he'd never been this near.

She crouched back in the shadows
Hoping that he'd go away
But Alfie wasn't leaving.
She was frightened of this stray.

Alfie ambled forwards,
Curiosity burned bright.
Perhaps this interloper
Would be spoiling for a fight.

But Purdy was too gentle.
Fighting really wasn't her.
Her owner wouldn't like it.
It would spoil her well groomed fur.

Alfie came much closer.
Purdy gave a quiet hiss.
He saw this pampered beauty
And said 'Well now, what is this? '

Purdy found some courage
And she met with Alfie's stare.
'I'm not out for trouble.
I won't fight you; wouldn't dare.

'I am just a house cat
Who needs time just to be free.
My life is one of comfort,
Yet I need time to be me.'

Alfie gave a chuckle,
'Don't be frightened. I won't bite.
But I would like to ask you,

Why did you come out tonight? '

Purdy talked to Alfie
And described the life she had.
She didn't want him thinking
That a house cat's life was bad.

She told him that she wandered
In the darkness as a treat.
Yet still she loved her comfy life,
So safe with lots to eat.

But now and then she liked
To take a wander in the night;
To feel the cool breeze on her
And to see the soft moon light.

Alfie listened closely
As she spoke of love and care.
He thought that being a house cat
Would be great with Purdy there.

He told her of his lifestyle;
Of his free and roaming ways.
Purdy listened to him,
Of his tough, uncertain days.

He walked her home and watched her
As they said their last goodbyes.
Then Purdy turned towards him
With a question in her eyes.

'Alfie, I just wonder,

Why not try a home that's yours?
My owners love all felines.
I am sure they'd help your cause'.

Now wind on to the future.
Alfie is a pampered cat.
Purdy's owners love him.
He is well fed, slightly fat.

He has a life of comfort,
Princess Purdy by his side.
Though night time still calls loudly,
And they both roam far and wide.

Their humans look on fondly
As the kittens round them play.
There never was a question
That their father, Alf, would stay.

But sometimes as it darkens,
As the kittens fall asleep,
They twitch as they are dreaming,
For the wildness still runs deep.

The Birth Day Angel

(for my wonderful parents)

One day the Birth Day Angel
Paid a visit to this land.
A baby soul was ready and
Her future must be planned.

The Angel came with questions
That the baby soul had asked.

With finding perfect parents
The Angel had been tasked.

Will you fill her childhood up
With happiness and love?
Meet any misdemeanours
With a guiding velvet glove?

Will you give her lessons in
What's wrong and what is right?
Will you both come running when
The monsters come at night?

Will you shape her character
And help her find her goal?
Will you feed her every need
In body, mind and soul?

Will you calm and soothe her
When she's sad and she is low?
And when it's time to leave you
Will you gently let her go?

But when the world is too much
And she needs somewhere to hide,
Will your door be open
With you waiting there inside?

The Angel passed the notes on
From each parent interview.
This baby soul read through them
And decided to choose you.

The Cottage In The Woods

There's a cottage in the clearing
In the woods down by the brook.
I often like to walk there
And I always stop and look.

The cottage is neglected,
Though I've never thought it sad.
They say, down in the village,
The old lady there is mad.

But I have seen her often
And I think that they are wrong.
She's at one with the cottage
Because she's lived there for so long.

The cottage has a garden,
Laid around it like a rug.
The flowers lean towards it,
In a bright, sweet scented hug.

The garden is not tended.
It is wild and it is free.
In fact, were I a flower,
It is where I'd want to be.

I've often seen the lady,
As I've stood and looked a while.
I've heard her whisper softly
And then give a gentle smile.

I don't know who she talks to
Or who she is smiling for.
But it seems the garden's listening
When she steps outside her door.

I've passed there in the winter
When a hoar frost grips the air.
And she's been in the doorway,
Talking, though there's no-one there.

And out there in her garden
Crystal threads run through the trees.
Frozen webs of silver,
Glinting brightly in the breeze.

In springtime I have seen her
Watch her garden re-emerge.
I've watched the green shoots pushing
Through the brown earth with a surge.

The winter webs now sparkle
With an early morning dew.
Washed down with April showers,
They look clean and fresh and new.

In summer she still whispers,
Though I've no idea to whom.
Yet I don't think she's crazy,
As the villagers assume.

The webs, now dry and silky,
Float in heady summer air.
The flowers in full glory
Seem to hold them with great care.

In autumn she stands gazing
As the leaves fall to the ground.
I see her lips are moving
But I cannot hear a sound.

The silken cobwebs hold fast
As the wind blows up a storm.
Below the mice and insects
Search for somewhere to stay warm.

Then as I stand there watching
From the place I stand each day,
She stops while in mid-whisper,
And she turns to look my way.

'I think you have a question,
Something that you'd like to know?
To whom is it I whisper
With my voice so soft and low? '

I nod, ashamed and worried
In case she should think me rude.
I'd hoped she hadn't seen me.
Never wanted to intrude.

Her eyes sweep round the vista,
Then she turns them back to me.
'Look around my garden,
Then describe what you can see.'

'I see your plants are wilting,
Ready for their winter sleep.
I see your cottage waiting,
Refuge from the snow, so deep.

'I see the leaves have fallen,
They are blanketing the ground.
I see so many creatures
As they scuttle all around.

'I see the lacy cobwebs
Wafting in the air like ghosts.
Artwork out of nature,
Framed with simple garden posts.

'I see a gentle lady
Who is at one with it all.
I watch her as she whispers,
In reply to nature's call.'

She holds her ageing hand out
And she bends close to my ear.
Then in a lilting whisper
Tells me what I want to hear.

'My garden is a canvas
Filled with wild and living art.
I cannot live within it
Without doing my small part.

'The silken threads lend romance,
Give an otherworldly feel.
They blur the lines and boundaries
Between fantasy and real.

'The spiders do the spinning,
For their work is oh so fine
I whisper patterns to them,
For my art is web design.'

The Perfect Kiss

The young and lonely princess walked
Along the riverside.
Her heart was filled with sadness
That her sweet face could not hide.

So many handsome princes
Had approached to take her hand.
So many kings had asked her
To be queen of their great land.

But none of them could see that
Her heart cried out for more.
None was her true soul mate.
Her heart hurt to the core.

She gazed across the river
And she gave a tragic sigh.
A tear ran down her soft cheek.
Another filled her eye.

Her raven hair fell forwards
And veiled her lovely face.
She sighed as she found solace
In so beautiful a place.

But beauty was her problem.

It was all her suitors saw.
They didn't care that inside
She offered so much more.

She longed to find a husband
Who loved her as a whole.
Who didn't just seek beauty
To fulfill a queenly role.

She cried and she lamented,
Wishing life could be more kind.
She hoped that somewhere out there
Was the love she wished to find.

Her tears ran to the river
And they joined the flowing stream.
They carried off her wishes,
They carried off her dream.

Downstream a frog was resting
On the sunny riverbank.
The warm rays made him thirsty.
He bent to the stream and drank.

The water was refreshing
And his thirst was well relieved.
It was more beneficial
Than the frog could have believed.

The magic in the water
Flowed down into his soul.
He knew with great conviction
He had to reach a goal.

But this frog was a stranger
To all matters of the heart.
He just could not imagine
How this poor frog was to start.

He knew his goal was true love

But it's object was unknown.
The frog must go out searching
So he would not be alone.

He travelled up the river,
Staying hidden in the reeds.
No-one could see him walking
Under cover of the weeds.

Then suddenly a sighing
And a sobbing reached the frog.
Fearful, he took cover,
And he hid behind a log.

He could not see the princess,
Though he heard her heartfelt prayer.
He wished not to disturb her.
She knew not that he was there.

'Please, somebody hear me.
Please can somebody take heed.
I'm feeling so unhappy.
Only one thing do I need.

I need someone to love me
Who will share in all my dreams.
To walk with me through long weeds
Down the banks of lovely streams.

I need someone who's gentle,
Who wants just a simple life.
A love I can grow old with
And not be his trophy wife.

I need a kindly person
Who is tender and sincere.
I want someone to love me
And to always want me near.'

The princess heard a rustle

From the weeds which grew nearby.
She looked and saw a frog there,
With a big tear in his eye.

She said 'Oh lovely creature,
You look sad as sad can be.
If I did not know better
I would say that tear's for me'.

The frog looked up in wonder
And he knew he was in love.
He smiled and slowly nodded
At the princess up above.

The princess smiled back at him,
And bent to give him a kiss.
The frog reached up towards her
To be sure she wouldn't miss.

The kiss was soft and gentle,
And delivered with such care.
All nature started singing
And sweet music filled the air.

Bright light shone all around them
As the magic spell took hold.
This was the kind of moment
Of which troubadors once told.

When the light had faded,
Sitting there upon two logs
In love and quite contented,
Were two very happy frogs.

The Sun Has Gone Out!

"The sun has gone out! "
I heard somebody shout,
"And someone must go up there and light it!

But where will we find
Someone who's of a mind
To take on this great task and ignite it? "

"It's not going to be me"
Said a dove in a tree,
"I'm a symbol of peace, not of power.
A hawk would be right
To take on such a flight.
He'd complete it in under an hour."

"True, I fly at great speed,
But for this job we need
Someone who can fly over great distance."
The hawk turned his head
To the swallow instead,
Who immediately showed his resistance.

"Perhaps I would be best
To take on this great test,
But I've just crossed an ocean to be here.
And my wings really ache,
Not much more can they take.
I might fail, and that's something we all fear."

A voice called out loud
From the back of the crowd,
"I'll give it a go. Let me do it."
A little brown bird,
Trying hard to be heard,
Said "Just give me a chance; you won't rue it."

Nobody there knew
What this plain bird could do,
But no-one else was volunteering.
Apparently, though,
This small bird didn't know
What the other birds there were all fearing.

So they gave him a flame,

Without asking his name,
They sent the brown bird on his travels.
Then as one they all said
"He is mad in the head!
What happens if all this unravels? "

But they shouldn't have fret,
For that brave bird was set
On setting the sun back on fire.
For although he was small
He was brave and had gall,
And those little wings would never tire.

As they gazed at the sky
They saw that, way up high,
The sun once again started blazing.
And as the sun burned
The wee brown bird returned
From his task. It was truly amazing!

As he reached the ground
All the birds gathered round
To welcome this hero returning.
He was home from his quest
With a wound to his chest,
Which glowed red where his feathers were burning.

What a hero he was,
And they loved him because
He was brave and faced danger for others.
And the burns he endured,
Though entirely cured,
Left their mark on his sisters and brothers.

When a Robin you see,
Somewhere up in a tree,
Give a thought to that brown bird before it.
For all birds will attest
That the lovely red breast
Was well earned by that first bird who wore it.

Singing Sands

A miracle of nature
In all ocean touching lands,
A wonder of the universe,
You'll hear the Singing Sands.

They sing their songs of wonder
To the rhythm of the sea.
They sing of all that there has been,
And what is yet to be.

They sing to children playing,
In the endless summertimes.
They sing them tales of mermaids
In their jaunty nursery rhymes.

And when the sea is stormy
They sing songs to bring it peace.
They soothe the angry ocean
Till the crashing waters cease.

Their songs tell tales of dancing
In the ever turning tide.
Their voices echo sweetly
All along the ocean side.

At sunrise and at sunset
In the ocean's doleful key
The sands sing songs of mourning
For all sailors lost at sea.

When Gargoyles Ruled The Earth

Way back in the mists of time,
Before the Earth had light,
An evil race of Gargoyles
Ruled the everlasting night.

Those beasts were evil to the bone,
Their skins infused with hate.
Their wickedness pulled all the Earth
Toward Hell's open gate.

The creatures of the world knew well
That Gargoyles were so cruel,
And silently they hid away,
So fearful of their rule.

The barren land, devoid of hope,
Was wilted, dark and bleak.
Plantlife, starved of love and light,
Was pitiful and weak.

While down below all nature hid
And cowered in the dark,
The Gargoyles swooped above the land
Which bore their evil mark.

Now and then the heavens tried
To send a spark of light.
But it was soon extinguished by
The terrors of the night.

The evil they exuded formed
A black veil in the sky.
The stars could not cut through the dark
No matter how they'd try.

Sometimes one star would break through
And shoot towards the Earth.
But darkness was a treasure

They'd defend for all their worth.

But one day out of nowhere
Nature howled a plaintive cry.
In utter desperation
They asked light for one more try.

With lightening bolts for swords they came,
And shields of burnished gold.
Mighty soldier angels were
A fine sight to behold.

They sliced through all the darkness,
Every cut was true and sure.
The black veil of the Gargoyles
Melted under light so pure.

Though the Gargoyles battled and
They fought with all their might,
The angel hoard were stronger and
They quickly won the fight.

They hurled the Gargoles downwards
Where they cast them into stone.
Held fast in the Earth's thick shell,
Eternally alone.

Millennia passed slowly
And the boulders held their wards.
The rocks concealed their secrets;
The imprisoned Gargoyle hoards.

The world around them flourished
'Neath the warm light of the sun.
The angels looked down proudly at
The work that they had done.

New species after species formed,
As only nature can.
Poured out in this new Eden,

Until one day there came Man.

Man strove hard for improvement,
He created his first tool.
He worked to gain advantage,
And then broke the ancient rule.

For following the battle
All Earth's creatures had agreed
To listen to the angels and
Heed what they had decreed.

They ruled that all the boulders must
Remain completely whole.
Imprisoning the Gargoyles was
To be their only role.

But Man's ideas were dfferent.
He thought that he knew best.
He embarked on a journey
To put this rule to the test.

He wanted to build castles
So he hewed out building blocks
From all the stones and boulders
And the Gargoyle prison rocks.

In doing so he weakened all
The magic that they hold.
The Gargoyles felt it falter and
Began to grow more bold.

As the time advances Man's
Ambitions grow and grow.
The Gargoyles get much stronger.
When the time is right they'll know.

The bonds of good which hold them
Get uch weaker, and they know
With one good push they'll surface

To take back the world below.

So look up at old castles.
They're not carvings that you see.
They're ancient evil Gargoyles
Who are straining to break free.

The Abandoned House

She wears her veil of cobwebs
With the shyness of a bride.
Her gown of moss and roses
Seal her glory days inside.

Her cataracted windows
Give no hint of what's within.
But as the house remembers,
So the magic can begin.

A million tiny dust motes
Float like bubbles in champagne.
The gentle laughter ripples
Through the empty halls again.

The swish of satin ballgowns
Sweeps away forgotten years.
The spirits of organza
Wipe away the house's tears.

To the spectral dancing
Of the ghostly candle light,
Unseen wraiths and phantoms
Play a waltz into the night.

Memories of heydays,
When the house was in full bloom,
Echo down the timeline
And replay in every room.

But time has done its damage.
Though the memories are good,
Her salad days are over.
She's just stone and rotting wood.

The bubbles are just dust motes,
And the swishing is just leaves.
The music, just a cold draught
As this once great manor grieves.

Pecking Order

I heard a small tap at the window.
At first I thought that I'd misheard.
But out on the sill there was pecking
A small and quite cross looking bird.

It turned it's small beady eye on me,
And wrinkled it's feathery brow.
I knew this was going to turn nasty,
So I said to him 'Ok what now? '

For this was a frequent intrusion.
This bird really liked to complain.
So, though I felt sure of the answer,
I asked 'Is it that moan again? '

The bird nodded then he launched into
His gripe in his usual way.
I knew before he started speaking
Just what that small whiner would say.

'It may have escaped your attention,
So I thought I would make it quite clear;
This feeder is totally empty.
There's no sign of bird food in here.

We birds turn up early each morning
To wake you up with a nice song.

You're breaking your side of the bargain.
For heaven's sake woman, what's wrong?

We sing some songs, then you feed us,
And we want a good hearty meal.
But often when we've sung our hearts out
You haven't gone through with the deal.'

I sighed and my heart grew quite heavy.
I'd heard this complaint many times.
This bird seemed to be the spokesperson
To point out my bird feeding crimes.

'Now look' I replied with impatience
'I'm not going to act like your slave
I'm going to come out now to feed you
But you must learn how to behave.

You all wake me up every morning.
I admit that I do love your song.
Does it have to be so very early?
I'm in need of a lie in that's long.'

The bird looked at me in confusion,
And said 'Now just wait a mo Dawn.
I've had a good look at your booking.
It says 'at sunrise every morn'.'

I said 'What was that you just called me?
Dawn certainly isn't my name.
But you've given a clue to our problem.
I think I know what is to blame.

Dawn lives half a mile along that way.
And if I'm correct in my hunch,
It's there you should sing the Dawn Chorus,
Then head down to me for your lunch.'

Don't Be Afraid Of Thunder

Don't be afraid of thunder.
I will tell the reason why.
Thunder is just road noise
That is coming from the sky.

To us the clouds are fluffy,
Like great balls of cotton wool.
But they're really water tankers,
And each one is very full.

They all have their own driver
Who must drive with special care.
For if they were to crash them
There'd be water everywhere.

Two companies employ them.
One owns dark clouds, one owns light.
Imps drive all the dark ones,
And each light, a Water Sprite.

Now, these two firms are rivals,
Each competes to be the best.
To distribute the raindrops
Is each tanker driver's quest.

The Sprites have happy natures.
In their light clouds they are calm.
But Imps are very grumpy,
And their dark clouds do the harm.

When they are widely spaced out,
Then their tempers do not clash.
But when they roll together
There is bound to be a crash.

So when you're looking skywards
And it's all dark clouds up high,
You know the driver Imps are in

A jam up in the sky.

For some time they'll be patient
And they'll try to wait their turn,
Be sure it won't be too long
Till their tempers start to burn.

And then they'll all start ramming
Into one another's cloud.
It's then it always rains hard
And the thunder is so loud.

A Matter To Decide

In a dark and empty nowhere
In no mortal time or space,
Four ancient thrones and table wait
For each to take their place.

Two Princes, two Princesses walk
With regal, high born pride,
Prepared to take their places with
A matter to decide.

A voice of great authority
Announced why these four met.
A matter of importance which
Was unresolved as yet.

'You gather at this table to
Decide which one is best.
You each may state why he or she
Should rule above the rest.

A King or Queen of Seasons, who
Is recognised by all.
A ruler of the Yearly Court
With power to enthrall.

Now, the first to tell you of
The benefits she'd bring.
I call the first contestant.
Please arise sweet Princess Spring.'

A young and childlike Princess rose
And tossed her golden hair.
The sweet perfume of springtime filled
The stale and musty air.

'Do not deceive yourselves that I
Am not as strong as you.
Whilst I am meek and gentle
I hold power to renew.

Prince Winter leaves a canvas which
Is bleak and all too bare.
I bring forth Mother Nature and
We plant a new world there.

I ask the sun to waken and
Direct his rays to earth.
I draw out shoots and creatures
And direct their sweet rebirth.

As animals and plants wake up
The whole world takes a breath.
Their homage is to Princess Spring
Who beats Prince Winter's death.'

Princess Summer rose with grace
And shone with golden light.
She looked at Princess Spring and smiled
'Sweet Princess, you are right.'

'It cannot be denied that you
Bring life back in your wake.
It's true that you are much loved,
But it's not for your own sake.

The world welcomes your coming
As it marks Prince Winter's end.
And I don't want to hurt you,
But the truth is harsh my friend.

You're loved because your coming shows
That I am on my way.
For everyone looks forward to
The first true summer's day.

Long and balmy evenings after
Hot and lazy days.
Carpets of wild flowers, bright
In sunshine's heat filled rays.

The sun shows his great power,
Mother Nature takes full bloom.
There is no doubt that Summer is
The most loved in this room.'

Prince Autumn stood and clapped his hands
And bowed at Summer's speech.
'Your words are true dear Princess,
But this crown's beyond your reach.

Although the whole world loves you
And they praise the joy you bring,
You cannot be our monarch
Any more than Princess Spring.

Summer is the season which
Shows Nature at her best.
But to achieve that beauty
Mother Nature must have rest.

Autumn brings a cooling and
Induces Nature's sleep.
I fill the earthly larders
What Spring sowed I now can reap.

A monarch must use power to
Meet every earthly need.
What greater show of love than
To give rest and richly feed? '

A fearful chill crept over as
Prince Winter took the stage.
The others pulled their cloaks close,
Ready to face Winter's rage.

'Prince Autumn sounds so noble as
He tells us of his care.
I can't deny the horror if
Prince Autumn wasn't there.

But, truth be told, he's merely there
Announcing my advance.
I hold back my invasion to
Give Autumn a fair chance.

A soldier, I come marching in
To weed out those too weak.
Mother Nature's general,
I make their small lives bleak.

If Princess Spring brings rebirth
It is my job to make room.
The strong need space to flourish so
The weak must meet their doom.

Emotionless crusader,
I bring coldness and take light.
But I bow down to any
With the strength to win their fight.

I clearly have the power to
Be monarch above all.
My weapon's fully ready to
Give answer to the call.'

The others gasped in horror as
They listened to his speech.
As one they knew the crown must stay
Out of this tyrant's reach.

The unseen Great Announcer called
For silence. As it fell
The Princes and Princesses each
Hoped that they'd argued well.

'Once more you all have stated why
Your regal claim is best.
You've also listened quietly
To claims from all the rest.

It's clear you all have passion for
The benefits you bring,
And clear you all have value,
Summer, Winter, Autumn, Spring.

I've come to a decision.
Not one of you is the best.
And therefore not one season
Shall be raised above the rest.'

In a dark and empty nowhere
Four great seasons gave a bow.
Bound all to rule together,
Each one swore a solemn vow.

Beware Bewaries

They nestle in the dusty bits
Beneath your bed by day.
At night they jump into your head
And with your mind they play.

Beware, they are Bewaries.
They were once a fairy race.

But due to bad behaviour they
Were banished from their place.

They're dark and sharp and spikey
And their voices sound like screams.
And while you sleep Bewaries like
To infiltrate your dreams.

Bewaries, unlike fairies,
Are not made of magic, pure.
They're made of something different
Something nasty, that's for sure.

When you have had a nightmare
And you suddenly awake,
The fear is quickly gathered.
New Bewaries it will make.

And every new Bewary
Is a nightmare to be had.
And thus they multiply and spread
And make your dreams go bad.

So if you are like me and feel
That good dreams are a must,
Don't harbour these Bewaries.
Keep your bedroom free of dust.

A Tale Of Two Buildings

You can call me Madam
I'm the Manor of these parts.
I had exquisite beauty
And I've stolen many hearts.

Five centuries I've been here
Upon my hillside seat.
Stood sturdy through the winters
And borne the summer heat.

I've hosted many parties.
Such glamour in my halls!
I've even welcomed Royalty
Within my stately walls.

I've loved each well bred tenant
Who lived with love in me,
But not the latest scoundrel
Who's selfish as can be.

I lost my much loved master
And passed down to his son,
Who laid waste to my treasures
To fund his betting fun.

To add to my misfortune
And rob me of my dues
A giant and ugly wind farm
Is planned to spoil my views.

As I survey my old stones
And stripped, neglected wood
I dream of what I'd do now
Were there a way I could.

I have a lighthouse cousin
On guard beside the sea.
I know if I could get there
He'd stand guard over me...

You can call me Captain.
I hold my head up high.
My job is to give warnings
As the ships and boats go by.

A lighthouse is the beacon
Which warns of hidden rocks,
So sailor's lives aren't threatened
As they make for their safe docks.

I used to share this duty
With men as brave as me.
Each one of them was hardy
And lived and breathed the sea.

Now I'm alone on duty.
Computers run my light.
No brave men live within me.
I'm lonely day and night.

Some engineers come monthly
To check for safety's sake.
They come by helicopter.
The noise makes my head ache.

Now I have lost my passion,
Though still wish sailors well.
But while my light's important
No-one loves it's shell.

I look to new horizons
Far from this coastal site.
Life with my country cousin?
To me that sounds just right...

Two once proud ageing buildings
Where once great purpose bloomed.
Now forced to face bleak futures.
Their foundations mean they're doomed.

A Cautionary Tale

The sleek Black Cat with emerald eyes
Crouched in the longer grass.
The unsuspecting Little Bird
Knew not what was to pass.

A breath of wind revealed the place

The feline was concealed.
The killer and the victim faced,
Fates finally revealed.

The glint of light on burnished claws,
The muscles tense and tight.
Razor teeth and iron jaws,
The Bird too shocked for flight.

"Please" said the Bird in whispered tones,
Although all hope was dead.
His little life was going to end.
It filled his heart with dread.

"What did you say? " the Black Cat asked.
The whisper made him pause.
"I'll let you make your plea to me
Before you feel my claws".

The Bird could not believe his luck.
A chance to make his case.
An argument he had to find,
His mind began to race.

"Nature has seen fit to give you
Power over me.
Your arsenal is much better
Than mine will ever be.

But as you plunge your teeth into
My fresh and tender skin
My death's upon me quickly.
So much slower for my kin.

My wife and children waiting
Will not live if left alone.
They'll starve and other predators
Will pick them to the bone.

I beg for your compassion.

I hope to make you see
That what is just a sport for you
Is tragedy for me".

With eyes closed and his head held low
The Bird drew in a breath.
The sleek Black Cat mulled over
If there should be a death.

The cat could see the reason for
Not taking this small life.
He held the power over this Bird's
Family and wife.

But just as words of mercy formed
Within the Black Cat's mind
The Bird became distracted by
A movement just behind.

A small brown Worm emerging from
It's home beneath the soil
Had left his wife and family.
For fresh food he must toil.

With casual indifference
The Bird pecked off it's head.
With mercy still on Black Cat's lips
He saw the Worm was dead.

Sleek Black Cat's bright emerald eyes
Slowly turned to slits.
Muscles taut, the Black Cat pounced
And tore the Bird to bits.

As Black Cat pulled the feathers from
His sharp and pearly teeth
He felt he'd dealt out justice
For Worm's family beneath.

Don't ever be a hypocrite.

Bird's tale should be your cue.
All weak and helpless creatures still
Have value just like you.

I Dreamed A Giant Marshmallow Dog

I woke from my sleep this morning
On the stroke of five.
I'd spent a fitful night.
I was just glad to be alive.

A giant white marshmallow dog
Had tried to eat my head.
Attempts to fight it off revealed
A pillow there instead.

But there, I've run away with things,
And started at the end.
I'll go to the beginning,
That's how a story should be penned.

I wandered in a garden with
White roses in full bloom.
Then suddenly I turned and saw
A massive sweeping broom.

It wasn't being pushed,
But it was sweeping on its own.
It swept a clear path for me
Where the plants were overgrown.

I followed where it led me.
Well, I had to, didn't I?
But then a big white cloud
Was falling gently from the sky.

It fell down with a splat.
That noise I clearly can recall.
I thought it would be quiet,

But I've never heard clouds fall.

The broom got quite annoyed.
It really didn't like the mess.
I understood its point.
It looked quite bad, I must confess.

The cloud began to move,
And as I stood there, quite agog,
I saw it change into a giant
White marshmallow dog.

I ran. It's what we'd all do
If a dream presented this.
Now, here's a really good bit.
Something you don't want to miss.

As I ran I saw ahead
A lake of chocolate sauce.
To try to swim through that
To get away made sense, If course.

Not for one brief moment
Did I think that I would fail.
I'd shake of this giant canine
That was chasing at my tail.

But as I leapt I saw
The chocolate sauce below had set.
As I crashed towards it did I panic?
Yes, you bet!

The giant white marshmallow dog
Was keeping quite good pace.
And as I landed with a jolt,
It landed on my face.

So now you know, when I awoke,
It was with some relief.
My head had not been munched upon,

As was my first belief.

I hope tonight, when I nod off
I am not going to find
A giant white marshmallow dog
There, waiting in my mind.

Grimoire

Mysterious Grimoire,
What secrets it holds
In the depths of its ancient
And yellowing folds.

Its beautiful cover
Of leather, so worn,
Was already old
When the heavens were born.

A stern golden lock,
Which does not have a key,
Stands as a guard
Keeping secrets from me.

To open this book
I must know the right word.
But it's never been spoken
And never been heard.

Mysterious Grimoire,
What power inside.
Is it good or pure evil
You faithfully hide?

Pressmennan Fairies (Part 1)

An Introduction

A dense and luscious Eden;
Rising slopes surround a lake.

Swans glide past serenely
Leaving ripples in their wake.

A tangled mass of plantlife
Dips along the water's edge.
A laughing small brook gambols
Till it tumbles down a ledge.

The trees stand tall and stately
As wild garlic gently sways.
A canopy of emerald
Shades meandering pathways.

The leaves, in whispers, rustle
To the buzzing of the bees.
A soundtrack of sweet birdsong
Plays from high up in the trees.

But hidden from the daytime,
And emerging just at night,
The woods will come alive
With creatures made from pure moonlight.

It's time to introduce you
To a wonder, a delight,
For sundown is the time
Pressmennan Fairies take their flight.

Tiny doorways open
In the trees down at the lake.
Small wings flit through cowslips
Trailing magic in their wake.

The fairies, fresh from slumber,
Dart from rowan down to fern.
Tending to the woodland
Is the fairies' one concern.

Each tree must be examined,
Every single blade of grass
Each bug trail must cleared

In case a beetle needs to pass.

But when the work is finished
Then the fairies get to play.
Enjoying all the freedom
That's denied to them by day.

Silver trails of moondust
Thread the velvet of the dark
Sapphire starlight sparkles
Fly up as the fairies lark.

And when their play is over
It is time for them to dine
On fresh bright rays of sunlight
And the sweetest honey wine.

The sunbeams, fresh and juicy,
Are caught in a web each day.
At dusk they're always harvested
Before they fade away.

The honey wine,
Delivered by the bees the day before,
Is left in drops of amber
Near each tiny fairy door.

And as the dawn comes creeping
On the far side of the lake,
The fairies know it's bed time
For so long they've been awake.

So welcome to Pressmennan.
It's a magic place, I know.
Like me, if you love fairies
It's somewhere you'll want to go.

Pressmennan Fairies (Part 2)

The Goblins Came

The autumn mist lay light and low
The day the Goblins came.
They'd laid to waste so many woods,
And here they'd do the same.

The hoard lined up upon the ridge
Above Pressmennan Wood.
They had one thought upon their minds;
To spill some fairy blood.

Below the fairy doors were closed,
Their dead bolts were drawn tight.
For fairies sleep till sundown
And the magic of moonlight.

The Goblins grew impatient,
Waiting didn't suit them well.
They hungered for destruction
Of this most enchanting dell.

With eyes to the horizon
They watched the darkness fall.
And as the sun retreated
They cried out their battle call.

They charged down to the lakeside,
Goblin claws tore at the ground.
The trees cried out in terror.
Oh, it was a tortured sound.

And as the ground was trembling
'Neath the hardened Goblin thugs,
The mud consumed the bodies
Of a thousand dying bugs.

The fairies heard the screaming

And they mobilised at speed.
Their woodland was in danger.
Mother Nature was in need.

They donned their acorn armour,
Pulling quivers o'er their wings.
They picked up bows of couch grass
And sharp arrows of wasp stings.

They summoned fairy magic,
Pulling power from the land.
The heavens held their breath to watch
Pressmennan Wood's last stand.

The clash was loud as thunder
As the fairies met their foe.
The Goblins screamed out orders
For the cold North wind to blow.

The fairies countered quickly
With a plea to all the trees
To spread their branches widely
And reduce it to a breeze.

They quickly fluttered skywards,
Gained advantage from their height.
They pulled back couch grass bow strings
And gave wasp sting arrows flight.

The Goblins roared in anger.
Fairies had the upper hand.
Destruction of Pressmennan Wood
Was not going as planned.

They tore at trees and flowers,
Ripping life force from their stalks.
They laid to waste all plantlife
And the shaded woodland walks.

They reached up to the branches

And they wrenched leaves from the trees,
The Great Voice of the Universe,
In booming tones cried 'FREEZE! '

A silence fell upon the woods.
A gentleness, a balm.
White and silver shimmered
As the Great Voice wove a charm.

He banished all the Goblins
To a distant Goblin hell.
He turned towards the fairies
And said 'Fear not, all is well.'

The fairies looked in wonder
At their devastated wood.
They saw the cold, white silver
Was a wondrous force of good.

The Universe spoke softly
'Pressmennan Wood has suffered so.
I've given time for healing
In the best way that I know.

The earth will sleep through winter
Safely blanketed in snow.
In Spring, when it's recovered,
Once again it all will grow.

But you, Pressmennan fairies,
Have a duty to perform.
Watch over your Pressmennan
Till the sun begins to warm.'

The fairies vowed that truly
They would do all that they could
To guard their precious Eden
And to heal Pressmennan Wood.

Pressmennan Fairies (Part 3)

A Sad Loss

The echo of the first drip
Shuddered through Pressmennan Wood.
A tiny patch of mud spread
Where the newborn snowdrop stood.

The brilliant white snow blanket
Turned to water in the sun.
The first drip found another
And the brook began to run.

The mirror on the surface
Of the lake just disappeared,
Melted by the sunrays
As the clouds of winter cleared

With darkness now approaching
And the rising of the moon,
Pressmennan Wood watched keenly,
For the fairies would wake soon.

A single silver moonbeam
Shone upon the woodland floor.
The first Pressmennan fairy
Opened up a tiny door.

Others followed quickly
In a rush of fairy dust,
No need now for the caution
That in winter is a must.

As one the joyful fairies,
Looking round began to sing
'The healing time is over
And it's time to welcome Spring.'

The trees and flowers,

Waking from their peaceful winter rest,
Rejoiced and started stretching
At their fairy friends behest.

The flowers started budding
On the woodland floor below.
The trees felt their leaves forming
As their roots began to grow.

Around them, fairies fluttered,
Gave encouragement in song.
Singing of their pleasure
To this living, breathing throng.

The moon glowed, strong and brightly
And the fairies worked for hours.
Bathing in the moonlight
They absorbed its magic powers.

And as the fairies tended
To each little bud and seed,
A chorus of sad voices cried
'There's someone here in need! '

The fairies rose and fluttered
As the bluebells rang alarms.
They gathered all their magic
And their strongest healing charms.

They flew in blurs of startdust
To where creatures gathered round.
And every single fairy
Shed a tear for what they found.

For lying in a glade they saw
The saddest sight to see.
There lay the lifeless body
Of a mighty old oak tree.

Pressmennan started weeping

At this most distressing sight.
The tears of plants and creatures
Mingled in the cool moonlight.

The loss of this great oak tree
Broke a thousand tender hearts.
The pain they feel cuts deeply
As another friend departs.

And so Pressmennan fairies
Carried out an ancient rite.
A spell of oldest magic
Rang out through the fading night.

The dawn was fast approaching
So this one chance they must take.
For as the magic ended
They would need the sun to wake.

Faded oak leaf spectres
Drifted in and out of view,
Weaving through the moonbeams
As they gathered morning dew.

They came to rest, and gently
Stroked the gnarled wood with this balm.
The fairies chanted softly
As they worked their magic charm.

As the enchantment ended
With the ghostly oak leaves gone
The fairy wings all fluttered
As the fairies sighed as one.

For there upon a lifeless branch
A single acorn grew.
That very precious infant would
Grow this old oak anew.

And then the far horizon lit.

The sun was on its way.
And we all know that fairies
Must be in their beds by day.

As the fairies slumbered
They were comforted by dreams.
The sun would bathe the acorn
In its nourishing warm beams.

Pressmennan Fairies (Part 4)

The Moon Cried

It was a summer of soft breezes
Sighing through Pressmennan Wood,
Blowing cooling kisses
Into every nook they could.

They'd gently ruffle feathers
On a duck or on a swan,
And coax the lake to ripple
Then they'd lazily move on.

The trees provided sunshades
From the glaring sun above,
Throwing dappled light
On every daisy and foxglove.

And somewhere in a clearing
Where an oak tree used to stand
There grew a thriving sapling
Tended by a fairy's hand.

This long and lanquid summer
Brought such beauty to this scene.
It shrouded scars with flowers
Where the Goblin hoard had been.

The days were so much longer

As the sun shone gold and bright.
The fairies' work was lessened
For they come out just at night.

As the clear sky reddened
And the sun slid out of view,
The fairies of Pressmennan
Came out, for the moon was due.

Transparent wings a-flutter,
They took flight, for they believe
That anything can happen
On a warm midsummer's eve.

They gathered in their harvest
For their special sunray feast,
Then left the sun their thanks to find
When it rose in the east.

With amber drops of honey wine
They gave the bees a toast.
A special thanks for bringing them
The drink that they love most.

They raised their faces to the sky
And hoped to see the moon.
Twilight now was fading
And it would appear quite soon.

They waited and they waited
Until minutes turned to hours.
Tonight they wished to laud the moon
For giving them their powers.

But still no moon appeared,
And then a star called down to say
'The heavens are in turmoil,
For the moon has gone away!

It gave a sigh this morning

Then it faded from the sky.
It didn't give a reason
And nobody here knows why.'

The fairies felt a panic,
For they knew, without the moon,
The magic they rejoiced in
Would start running out quite soon.

'Oh moon, why have you left us? '
Was the fairies' plaintive call.
Then gently from above them
Salted tears began to fall.

A silver voice in darkness
Whispered 'You do not need me.
The sun has blessed your summer.
He's the one you want to see.

I've watched from here in sadness,
And I know that I'm not wrong.
The moon is not required
When the summer days are long.'

Pressmennan gasped in horror
At the musings of the moon.
They loved this astral dweller
As it brought a magic boon.

A song passed through the woodland
To the moon up in the sky.
A song of praise and wonder
And the fairies gave a cry.

'Oh moon, you're made of magic.
Nothing else can take your place.
For you're the one sustaining
Our blessed fairy race.

We love the sun, of course we do,

We love the warmth it brings.
But, moon, you are the only one
For whom Pressmennan sings'.

With a sparkle of soft moon dust
The moon gently reappeared.
As magic rays caressed them
The Pressmennan fairies cheered.

The sun and moon decided
That they both need time to rest.
They shared their time for shining
As the summertime progressed.

With autumn fast approaching
The fairies filled their stocks
In golden barrels, sunshine.
Moonrays in a silver box.

The trees, the plants and creatures
Rejoiced as both of them shone.
The story turned to legend
Of the Night The Moon Was Gone.

Pressmennan Fairies (Part 5)

The Wind Blew

The gentle breeze of summer,
Which had brought a cooling bliss,
Turned traitor in the autumn
With its cutting Judas kiss.

It roared along the valley
Causing waves upon the lake.
It rampaged through the woodland
Causing smaller trees to break

Pressmennan Wood stood bravely,

Trees gave shelter where they could.
The Fairies searched for magic
To protect their precious wood.

And then, one night at sundown
As the wicked North Wind surged,
The tiny doors flew open
And the Fairy folk emerged.

The wind screamed out in anger
As the fairies took to flight.
It swept them through the woodland.
Magic sparkles lit the night.

The trees spread out their branches,
Snatching fairies from the sky.
They knew they must not lose them
Or Pressmennan Wood would die.

The woods around grew silent
As the north wind took a pause.
The fairies must act quickly
Before it resumed its roars.

They looked at all the damage
Caused to their beloved wood.
They sprinkled healing magic
Over everything they could.

They tended to the branches
Of the trees, their strong limbs stripped
Of all their autumn glory
As the wicked north wind whipped.

They soothed the weeping willows
Bowed in terror by the lake.
They swept across the water
Leaving calmness in their wake.

And as they flew, their magic

Trailed and glittered in the night.
It swirled in rainbow colours,
Weaving with the moon's soft light.

The north wind gazed in wonder
At the love it saw below.
The magic quelled its anger,
And it lost the need to blow.

Pressmennan Wood was sleeping
When at last the north wind left.
But it had suffered badly,
And the fairies were bereft.

As they surveyed the damage
To their beloved wood,
They noticed, in the carnage,
The pine trees bravely stood.

Standing straight as guardsmen,
Solid, strong and green.
They had not been stripped bare
As other trees had been.

The pines could still give shelter
To birds till spring arrived.
Enfolding and protecting,
Ensuring they survived.

The fairies asked the pine trees
To stand sentinel till spring,
To guard the woods through winter.
To watch over everything.

They cast some gentle magic
Above their lovely dell.
Pressmennan Wood grew peaceful
As enchanted snow flakes fell.

The fairies slept in day time,

But still went to work at night,
Each one assigned a pine tree
To protect with fairy light

If you should pass Pressmennan
I know you will want to stop
To gaze upon these pines,
Each with a fairy light on top.

ABOUT THE AUTHOR

I see poetry and stories in everything and everywhere. The world of imagination is a beautiful and wondrous place. I hope you have enjoyed your visit to mine.

Judith

Made in the USA
Columbia, SC
28 May 2017